Poems:

Images Through Words

NOREEN RAE COOK

Ten|16
PRESS

www.ten16press.com - Waukesha, WI

Poems: Images Through Words
Copyrighted © 2022 Noreen Rae Cook
ISBN 9781645383536
First Edition

Poems: Images Through Words
by Noreen Rae Cook

For information, please contact:

www.ten16press.com
Waukesha, WI

Cover and interior artwork by Noreen Cook
Cover design by Shannon Ishizaki & Kaeley Dunteman

Dedication:

For my three children, Richard, Susan, and Paul. And with thanks to my family and friends who have sustained and encouraged me over the years.

Note:

This collection of poems begins in 2013, when Noreen began writing on her iPad. This became her norm, as she loved her Apple devices and all they connected her with.

Contents

Chapter 1:

Before

Life after 80?

So quaint, so cute, so useless
Those 80-something women
No adjective for their lives
Alone, mostly
Memories of no value, skills of no value
Once good wife, good mother, good housekeeper
Now surrounded by loss
At the moment when life becomes
A supernova of light, color
Understanding, compassion, comprehension
Unable to share
Inarticulate Joy.

February 5, 2013

Ode to my iPad

At last, the friend I've dreamed of!
Always at hand
Dreamy gift from above
In retirement land.

February 5, 2013

Mystery

No more mysteries
No bowling ball to create thunder
No chariot of fire to bring the sun
No angel wings to drop the snow.

Am I happier without those tales
Let imagination create an image
That made the world a story
We could understand.

Or were we supposed to move
From wild story to cold fact
In order to see the new mystery
Of kindness, love, compassion?

March 2013

Sorry!

I am sorry I grew up with loving parents,
With food, home, family,
With school, books, music
And you did not.

I am sorry I had church every Sunday,
Huge family gatherings every holiday,
Teachers who cared
And you did not.

I am sorry that Justice has not
Rolled down like a mighty river
And swept away those differences
To take away "you did not."

I know these things and yet
Each morning my heart sings
With the promise of the new day
And you will too.

March 21, 2013

Terrible two?

She stamps her feet and slams the door
Commands, demands pour from her lips
Her lovely hair flies wild about,
A deadly furrow cuts her brow.
Her eyes send poisoned arrows
And her voice turns wild and sour.
Embarrassed, those who love her
Stand silent and ashamed
For her. She's over 50
When will she leave this game?

May 23, 2013

The gift

You might think the gift had cost a million dollars
Or taken years to produce
With gold, paint ground from
Earth's rarest stones.
But not at all.
It was a simple invitation to view the lake at sunset.
A quick drive from the silent suburb
To the public beach
Where young and old, fit and infirm, sweat-shining skin
Shone in the long evening rays.
Life, joy in all its glory
Reflected in our faces.

August 2013

For New York

To see, to feel, to hear, to breathe
thousands of sensations at one time.
To love the doorman, the cab driver,
the waitress, the policeman at the corner.
To find home in your hotel room after
a day of emotional highs
when you felt the great buildings,
paintings, stolen artifacts of the whole world
packed into this magnificent city.

To return to the familiar places,
faces, smells, rooms of home
but not you, never again you,
because New York has changed
who you are and who you want to be:
a citizen of the whole world, of the
changing exciting chaos of life,
fully human and loving it all.

October 2013

Family and the Kitchen

The kitchen is the center of life
In some family traditions.
Not just food prep but
Intimate conversations, safe ones,
Sharing thoughts while looking
Efficiently busy.

But not all families are the same,
Is that a surprise?
And the kitchen belongs to the wife,
Maybe an evolution from
A time when there was little else
That she controlled.

Stay out of my kitchen.

An appearance of serene control,
Food appears, clutter is hidden,
Changed roles from family to
Guest.
But what is lost?
Family and guests do not open
Their hearts and minds.
While separated
Knowing each other is lost.

November 6, 2013

Seamus Haney missed the point

Seamus Haney missed the point in his poem "Blackberry Picking."
He is right about the hot sun, the scratched arms,
The delicious purple stain on shirts, fingers, lips,
The ping of berries falling into empty cans.
His grief that the berries did not last.
What he missed (one wonders about his upbringing)
Coming home hot and tired but . . .
Picking the berries clean of bugs and leaves . . .
Baking fresh blackberry cobbler topped with golden cream,
The bubbling pot of blackberry jam
Waiting for sparkling glass jars
Stored for winter mornings,
Taking the blue bowl filled to the brim with black gold
To the neighbor next door.
And falling to sleep, still sticky and sweet,
Content.

March 14, 2014

The soul needs snow

The soul needs snow.
The covering up of all
Earth's colors,
Symbols of human passions—
Hatred, greed, lust.
Snow in its purity talks of
Serenity, compassion, contemplation.
A reminder of who we
Truly are

November 16, 2014

30 shades of gray, or the yellow bus

The school bus driver, a kind man,
Pulls up as close to the cars as he can
Car doors open, orthotic shoes reach out
To find the pavement before stepping out
Spindly legs, heavy coats, gloves and scarves
Around wattled throats.
Up three steps, handrail of course,
Narrow aisle, kids size of course.
Two by two, careful and slow
They find a seat in an empty row,
Clutching a purse, ticket in hand,
Carefully curled gray heads bend
To each other.

Passing by, you see the gray
Heads, scorn for them begins to play
Through your mind but then
You think, will I have the courage when
I am old and gray, to still find seat 13k,
listen to my orchestra play
Beloved music, I am still alive
And go about, enjoy, rejoice, thrive.

May 24, 2015

Rites of Passage, American Style

They are so powerful,
Pictures of boys waiting
To be introduced, through painful
Rituals, or dangerous trials,
into the world of men.

No ambiguity there!
The whole world knows
You belong.

But we decided
A smattering of small formal steps—
Baptisms, graduations, licenses—
Promised inclusion
Into our smaller world.

Does your heart long for
That single celebration?
The assurance of belonging
Completely in your world
Forever.

December 20, 2015

The Last Extinction

Thank you.
I thought I knew you
I've watched you grow
For twenty years
Accepted expected stages
Loving laughing worrying.
But
Unscheduled time and
At last we found
A truthful moment
To reveal a new world
Of values, words, beliefs.
And
As a candle in a dark room
Beams light on hidden corners
Your words brought light
New thoughts, new life
into my world.

December 21, 2015

Alone, Together

I thought, I felt, I knew
The pattern of my life
Family, marriage, children
Their families, marriages, children
The elemental longings
Repeated over and over.

Minutes, hours, days, years
Sharing, growing, endless exploring
Until a crack appears . . .
Strange words, different vision
Straining the connecting thread.

And then awareness of
Another elemental truth
I am and always have been
Alone.

December 21, 2015

In the woods

I find in the woods
A tiny shard of
Broken mirror.
Surround by bits of soft green moss
And it becomes a tiny lake.
Acorn caps for bowls
And twigs for a tiny forest
Hollyhock ladies
With hollyhock turbans
Exotic and beautiful
Dance on the lush floor.
The only sound
wind and bird call
A child
Alone in the woods
Could dream.

February 2, 2016

The kids are coming!

The kids are coming
Head for the store
olives and bread
Wine and truffles.
Just for one night
But better than none.
Perhaps a moment
To touch each other.
These faces are like
The old gods, bringing
Joy and awe, a brief glimpse
Of Paradise.

February 3, 2016

Diploma

In a plain brown envelope
I found a treasure
Cream and scarlet and gold
A piece of paper
But a symbol of
Four years of life,
study, fun and music.
A passage to the future
Surrounded by love.

May 14, 2016

April Snow

At last a silence comes
Deep as the new snow
Clean, untouched, soft

At last, rest for the ears
And eyes and mind
From constant whirl

At last, time freed
Nothing must be done
Today except glory

In the great gift of
Quiet for meditation
On why.

April 16, 2018

Old Photos

An old photo, black and white
A young girl, white dress, hair pulled into a bun,
Her face calm, eyes downcast, hands folded
My grandmother . . .
My grandmother was old, fat, hair in a braid around her head,
An ally against my mother, a cake baker,
A porch sitter, never a young woman with dreams.
Now I am the old one, trying to understand
How I became me, what do I owe her
That young woman in the white dress
Who I never knew.

March 18, 2019

After the astronomy lecture

I turn out the light about 10:30, open the patio door, scurry under the blankets and then I look at the sky where for the past 4 nights, the moon has waned away from a perfect round to a slice and has slowly moved across the window . . . wait, wait, I am the one who is moving, my shadow is eating that glorious serene ball. Time after time I must catch myself and look with clear eyes.

We and everything in our world resulted from an explosion long long ago, hot gases, colliding particles, collapsing and recombining, creating all the elements of our life. And we are only one of many galaxies, other life to be discovered as science becomes more powerful.

It is the explosion of technology—microscopes and telescopes— ever more powerful destroying the myths we use to explain what we do not understand. And creating another gulf between people at a time when understanding and loving our neighbors is as important as anything we must do in order to remain human at least as I define that word.

In the past, when people actually talked about sin, despair was considered one. I am beginning to understand why; it creates lethargy, immobility, gray world, retreat . . . all a blanket to hide beneath. In order to stay loving and caring and empathetic, one must decide to be all those; it is a decision I can conscientiously make when each day begins.

March 27, 2019

I saw my daughter

I saw my daughter dancing with her son
Steps with names like 'swim' and 'mashed potato'
No waltz or foxtrot, bodies in constant motion
Faces serious and smiling,
Flushed and joyous.
A sense of serenity came over me
If I need a purpose for life
This might be as close as I ever come to finding it
Late at night, in the kitchen, after a holiday meal
My connection to eternity.

December 27, 2019

Chapter 2:

Covid Time

That kind of snow, you know

March and longer light
Green shoots pushing through icy dirt
Birds searching for bits of thread and
Rabbits chasing through the bushes.

Every year, unexpectedly,
or maybe awaited

The last snowfall happens
Usually at night and when light comes
Each branch and twig, wire and walk
Are exquisitely painted,
Just so we can remember the
Beauty bred in our bones.
It is that kind of snow, you know.

March 23, 2020

2020 in 20 words

Weary of "crisis, horrible, tragedy"
Where did "love, hope, honesty"
Go?
Like leaves hidden under the snow

July 7, 2020

Hang Nail

My finger is going over and over
This sore place. I know it will hurt
But welcome that sharp short pain
Until finally I bite the offender away.
Ideas seem the same . . . there they are
Every quiet moment, demanding attention.
Round and round my thoughts go
A spiral, closer and closer to an answer
And suddenly it seems clear—I was wrong!
My assumptions put me on the wrong track
Start over with a clear mind and a good heart.
"An unexamined life is not worth living." Thoreau?

July 7, 2020

Time

Like clockwork . . .
Sunday morning meant
Smell of shoe polish, curled hair, ribbons.
Sunday School, Church,
The smell of roasted meat and vegetables,
Pie, a drive into the countryside
Ice cream for supper! Perfect Sabbath.

Sunday morning, August 2020
Coffee and toast while reading email, NYT online,
An hour in the pool for exercise,
Family Zoom, faces and voices out from space
Leftovers, neighbors waving as they pass by
And finally, 10 and I can go to bed.
Life was overflowing in luxury and ease so
Why is my soul uneasy, my mind unsettled?
What do you know that still makes sense?

August 2, 2020

Ruth Bader Ginsburg

In the past, when a hero died
The great poets, statesmen and philosophers
created magnificent works honoring that
Unique human.
"Oh Captain, my Captain"
"When lilacs last in the dooryard bloomed"
"Sail on, oh ship of State"

Our hero saw, with omniscient clarity.
Our hero gave her life to share her vision,
A country growing in understanding and
Without exception, demanding Justice for all.

Incredible idea! Impossible dream! Wishful thinking!
And yet, my life has changed because of her
Before, I was "and wife" on documents
She gave back to me my name.

September 21, 2020

RBG II

One life, one hero, one champion who spoke
The truth, who convinced others to believe
Equality is possible. Justice is possible.
Magnificent works to honor our RBG
Must be written, spoken, read, published,
NOW.

September 21, 2020

The Painter

Golden sky, splash of orange mixed w/ gold,
Shades of blue, red, yellow
The spectrum in all its varieties.

The painter starts with flowers—
Color and shape are familiar.
Next a farm or country landscape—
Hills, fields, glimpse of water.

Then abstraction, I demand from you
. . . any emotion, any physical response.
It tells me I might be on the right track.
We are together!

September 28, 2020

Surface Tension

Drops of rain, perfectly round.
How can that be? What keeps them together?
The knowing speak of physics
But in my heart, I know, it is
Love.
Fragile as a spider web,
When beliefs clash in families
loving surface tension keeps the circle
Perfectly round.

Fear, confusion, uncertainty,
Balance has disappeared from our world.
And yet our life goes on,
surface tension holds us in love.

September 28, 2020

Why words once had meaning

Words once had meaning.
Quadratic equations or regression analysis
are now a foreign language.
But images are stark and clear.
Plato's cave,
Infant Achilles held at his ankle,
Forever vulnerable.
Book titles, authors' names disappear
Like smoke
But the plight of the Bennett girls
Is clear.
Nothing seems to be a rock on
Which everything stands,
Except
every human longs to find meaning
For their life. Stories are cracks in our
Narrow minds allowing new ideas, emotions,
To challenge what we are.

October 5, 2020

I Am Turning to Stone

I am turning to stone
I am turning to stone
First toes, then fingers
Ankles, wrists.
This can't have a happy ending.

So many blows to the things I believe . . .
I can keep my family safe . . . no
I can convince the unbelievers . . . no
I am relevant, responsible . . . no

With each loss, another body part goes.
I watch this happen, curious but not fearful.
To expect exemption from peril denies my
Humanness.
God does not ration joy or sorrow.
We decide.

October 6, 2020

"She must go home or she will die," the Doctor said.

"She must go home or she will die," the Doctor said.
"Her Mother, Father, sisters, brothers, the mountains
Are her life blood," he said.
And so she did,
go back home for a while
but then her new life found her soul
And she went home, started again.

Separation is always part of our life story,
Nostalgia always there, perfect past.
Hardships, pain, suffering fade with time
Memories—joy, love, beauty—survive to
Sustain, no matter how faint,
Hope.

October 17, 2020

This is the Day

Early morning lights the sky
Hot coffee and toast, mail and news,
Light and heat, water and food
What possible fate gave these to me?

Because if I
hear the wailing children trapped
see the ruined cities, smell the burning world,
stay safe at home, do nothing
Am I human/humane? Hell is waking to a world gone mad
While family, work, pleasure kept
Awareness away . . .
Till today. Now what?

October 26, 2021

Cinderella's Other Story

I say,
"Sorry, Cinderella, there is no Fairy Godmother.
In fact, there is no Prince Charming either.
The life you have is real and
Dreams fade in the sunlight."

She pleads, "That is not fair.
I play by the rules, am kind,
Love my neighbors, help others.
And still my life is hard.
What more can I do?"

I need an answer but what?
"Living is the gift, the world is the gift,
Every living being could be the gift.
Your life is your creation
Savor it all."

November 1, 2020

Daylight Savings Time

An arrogant idea, that we can save time
As if it is simply another commodity
We control.

We know why it rains or snows,
What causes thunder or lightning,
We accept.

But
Saving time means doing more
Doing more means we are valuable
We are worthwhile.

The sense that we are simply
One among many, dying as we breathe
Is the final truth.

November 1, 2020

Looking for work

I can . . .
turn flour and butter into delicious products
wash bedding and clothes, from hot suds to blueing rinse and hang
out to dry, underwear discreetly hidden from view
starch and iron shirts and smocked dresses till they are as
smooth as silk
feed a family of 5 on a can of tuna, mushroom soup and peas
manage to have three children, clean, polished, shined and ready
for church every Sunday morning
comfort a child, whether sick or simply buffeted by the world,
read together at bedtime no matter how tired

go to Ladies Aid, PTA, Cub Scouts, Boy Scouts, Indian Guides,
Brownies, Girls Scouts, League of Women Voters, Choir practice,
Open Housing Marches, bake sales, potluck suppers
Bridge Club, Book Club, Coffee Klatches,

create a clean orderly home with pleasure and pride

Please reply if you need any of these services.
Sincerely,
Mom

November 4, 2020

Anguish

I know this word but till today
When it broke my heart, and
Its meaning entered my soul
Can I truly use the word.

Religions try to prepare us
For the moment when life
Crashes, crushes, destroys
The perfect world we made.

Words, music, art have
Warned that this will come.
Grief, so long avoided, arrives
And everything else evaporates.

In the darkness, turmoil, confusion
I search for anything to help me.
Then remembering my past
And present filled with love

I will go on.

November 5, 2020

Olympics, 2016

I never dreamed that I could play
Boys' sports. Their bodies were
So strong, so supple, so powerful
And I was just a girl
Assigned to admire and praise.
Jacks, jump rope, hopscotch—
I excelled in those wearing my cotton dresses
Hair neatly brushed, hands and face clean.

Today
Watching volleyball on the beach,
Beautiful strong graceful bodies
Leaping and diving and punching
My joy in these young women
Is tempered by a longing to
Start over today when
I would be on that team
Glorious in mind and body.

Why do I need to know?

Why do I need to know where you are?
In which room, on which chair
With which cup and book?
A mind dulled by months of isolation
Separated from all those whose
Love made life worth the struggle.

Remembering tales told by the
Old ones . . . leaving, leaving,
Leaving homes and mountains,
Lakes and rivers,
The hardest part always
Leaving friends who knew them.

Am I less than they were?
Their stoic acceptance of loss
Their courage to start over, again
And again and again. The tie that
Binds also lifts the spirit
In gratitude.

November 29, 2020

I knew who I was

I knew who I was before . . .
My name, my birthdate, my family
I knew my children, their homes,
Addresses and phones.

12345, 54321, ABCDE4321, ZWXY1234.
Someone decided I needed more
Letters/numbers/symbols to
Prove me!

Have I become less or more?
Can numbers prove I am me?
If I forget the codes, have I gone
Away into a cloud overhead?

A neighbor waved and smiled
A friend sat 6' away on the patio
I found an orange at the door
Something is still here simply
Waiting.

December 16, 2020

Speaking on the condition of anonymity

(It's hubris to claim to know)

This glorious world we see
Confirms our immortality

Since first our eyes were opened
The blazing sun, the sky
Forests, oceans, critters
Flood the mind's eye

With amazement, love and joy
Arrives the staggering thought
We have everything we need
This world is gift enough.

Parting the Red Sea, stopping the sun
Bringing the dead alive, feeding 5000 with
One loaf, why do these tales
After hundreds of years still tell us a truth?

Could it be miracles change us, how we see
Our world, the ancients sending a message
"look deeper into yourself" for answers.

December 16, 2020

Cookies

Time to find the battened recipe book
Pages spattered with stains, limp,
Loved.
Spritz—the dough caught in the press
Or clinging to the cookie sheet, misshapen
Trees or wreaths, red cinnamon star on top.
Toffee Bars—butter crust, chocolate layers
Chopped nuts on top.
Peppermint Patties—pungent smell, dipping
Into tempered chocolate.
Pfeffernusse—dark brown dough full
Of spices.

"Unhealthy" my friend shouts, and of course
She is right, sugar and butter.
So why do I wait eagerly for the box?
Because this is food for the soul!

Baking together, time without interruption.
Memories, years of tradition in a small bite.
I am more than this moment. Baking
At Christmas will connect us forever.

December 29, 2020

Change

Why do I resist change when I know
CHANGE is the only permanent in life?

I wear my old bathrobe, not my new one.
My old shoes find their way to my feet
My car is a 2001, my bookshelves are filled
With old favorites, my style is 'classic.'

Still my new motto is "Adapt or Die"
New authors, artists, classes, and
Especially new eyes. *A Different Mirror**
Is breaking down walls I never saw.

And this is the exciting thing . . .
I feel lighter, cleaner, buoyant
The future will be better because
We are stronger than we knew.

A Different Mirror, Ronald Takaki

January 11, 2021

Reality

Sometime in the distant past
I saw a bumper sticker
"If you think education is expensive,
Try ignorance."

And here is an interesting fact
Many of our leaders have degrees from
Prestigious colleges, many are lawyers.
They have impressive educations.

What is the missing element in their lives
That clouds judgment, compassion,
Love. Their humanity has evaporated
As their prestige grows.

Enigma, the decoding genius from WW2
Looks at chaos and by some magic spell
Finds the thread that gives meaning.
This might be the gift of Covid
Time to find that thread.

January 15, 2021

"Little things mean a lot"

An old song from an old world
With a new resonance.
During the months we are apart
Little things are the greatest loss.
Baking in the kitchen together
Walking the 'circle' together
The house and table filled with
Family and friends.

Nostalgia for the past just for a moment.

Re-vision, seeing anew, is a gift
This time gives us. Rose-colored glasses
Are gone, a magnifying glass is here.
We can begin to make our dreams real
We can change our minds and hearts,
Alleluia!

January 22, 2021

Reprieve

In isolation, time has a unique space
Each day could melt into the next
Only night is sure.
I wait for dawn, black, gray, ash,
Light!
The plan to create (write-draw-paint-
Bake-cook-clean-discard-exercise)
Dissolves in the light.
And then, suddenly an expected delivery is cancelled
A surge of relief, freedom, release . . .
Once again nothing is expected, awaited.
Another endless day that I fill
Carelessly as though I have all
The time in the world!

January 26, 2021

Can you imagine

Can you imagine how it feels
When the documentary talks about your memories
As though they were in another world?

Can you imagine how it feels
To have your loved ones spoken of
As casualties of some distant past?

Can you believe you will be blamed
For omissions made while you were
Learning who you might be?

And can you believe your life
Your special essence will be
Simply a note in an essay?

February 8, 2021

Covid puzzle

Like a raptor circling above the snow
Watching for any trace of a mouse,
My fingers are poised above the keyboard
Waiting, waiting for the signal to join
The elect.

It moves, I hit the key, it asks for
Information, more, more,
And then with disdain says,
"No appointments for a month."

A miracle (my life is full of them)
Grandson in Boston was also
Circling, pouncing, adept
And tomorrow I join those few
Who hedge their bets with
Science.

February 15, 2021

Do you wonder?

What is happening to 'us'?
Will we be able to read a face
Give meaning to tone, inflection
To touch the human soul
Reaching out for confirmation.

Almost a year without a hug,
I see a half face, half expression
Hear only words without connections
To meaning, desires, sorrows,
Reality Life is slipping away.

Or this may be our real world
Forever, longing to share the
New vision, the work that
Needs to be done in creation
Incomplete till shared.

February 20, 2021

Hope

"Calm down, don't get so excited,"
The weatherman said, "more cold is coming."
But by then joy has escaped,
Harder to control than the virus.

Snowy tracks become puddles,
The lumpy white sheet out my window
Becomes a lacy tablecloth
And then . . . my yard!

Pure oxygen flows through the
Open door, breath becomes life,
Cells, blood, nerves wake, gulp
And remember why they live.

Thousands of years and this day
Never changes.
Persephone bringing her daughter
Home, inexpressible joy.

February 23, 2021

Reversal

My daughter sends me cookies
My Grandson checks my food,
My sons FaceTime and call me
My Sisters text their mood.

Before, I did the calling, kept
The family tie "that binds"
Followed every celebration
Knew how connections find

A common touch of love
Across a thousand miles.
I was the anchor in the chaos
Till you came and with a smile

Cut the chain and freed me
Someone else can care
Enough to clear the pathway
While I float in dreamy space.

February 26, 2021

Question

Maybe we're not created
To see before our eyes
Rolling scenes of horror,
Cruelty, hatred, meanness,
Madness really. They stay there,
Crowding out real life.

Maybe we're not created
To see before our eyes
Beneath the sea, above the earth,
Into cold black outer space
Deserts, jungles, glaciers,
Millions of stars.

Maybe we were created
To see only beauty, love,
Compassion and care
This might be our worldview
A re-vision we can hold.

March 3, 2021

From Marsha, wife of Marcus Aurelius

"You know I love Marcus, but a word to the wise . . .
To be a Stoic (and my husband is the best of the lot) you must
have a wife! Marcus starts his day aligning himself in the universe.
I, on the other hand, start mine before he gets up so his tea is
ready by 5 a.m. Breakfast for the children, boys off to school and
I am teaching our girls so classes all morning. Marcus has invited
his friends for dinner; I am considered a good wife so his friends
love coming to our house (often!) for meals and though the slaves
cook the meal, I plan the menus and shopping lists. My days are
filled keeping up appearances: sparkling togas, personal grooming
because he is careless about that, social contracts so he can stay in
power, care for both our parents . . . the list is endless. I am tired of
your adulation for him. What about me?"

March 6, 2021

What do those ancient stories mean

What do those ancient stories mean
When meals served slaughtered children?
A warning-revenge creates animals?
Always Furies are waiting in the wings
Wild, whirling chaos, cruel death.
Unknowing parents eating their child

I read the ancient
Tales, shudder at them.
They ate their children!
How cruel, barbaric,
Un-natural.
But
Now we are so civilized
We offer them up
In bits and pieces—
How smart they are,
How creative they are,
How misunderstood they are.

March 6, 2021

Do you remember Cassandra

Do you remember Cassandra?
Beware of the glib, the smooth talkers
Those who offer simple solutions.
Where are our truth-tellers?

I do not want to hear that I,
(Comfortable, listener to public radio,
Member of a social action church,
Doner to music, libraries, art,
Charities . . . frugal, green, liberal.)
I AM the problem!

I have so much, luxury unimaginable.
While most of my sisters suffer
Without hope.
Frozen, caught in the net of my own
Selfish comfort, unable to act
When I know, sense the depth
Of my complicity in the
Tragedy of this time.

March 7, 2021

Does it matter that you, my beloved:

Does it matter that you, my beloved:
Will never pick wild raspberries in the hot summer sun
Smell the rich ripe juice, savor the warm wine flavor.

Will never, having finished your chores, hear
"Go out and play but be home at supper time"
And head for the lake or woods, free at last.

Will never wander through the woods
Finding treasures—wild flowers, a feather, a dead bird
And creating a funeral,

Will never walk to school
Scuffling dry leaves, splashing in puddles,
Making tracks in new snow,
whispering

March 7, 2021

Summer mornings

Absolute stillness . . . no echoing machines filling empty spaces in my mind
Even the birds seem hushed after a raucous work week
And no flickering shadows behind closed curtains.
Sun shadows stream across the floor, touching, searching, growing.
"Go out, go out; this is a gift freely given"

March 7, 2021

Shocked!

      I wonder why I am always shocked
When stories rise thru the cacophony
Of every day, stories that reveal 'me.'
I pretend I have always been
on the side of justice, I have always
Taken the right path,
I have never turned away.
      Reality says the screen in my eyes
Has kept me from seeing. Now, how can
I go on, bearing the suffering of women
of Syria, Yemen, the world??
Complicit in every 'shocking' act
By looking away?
      Being shocked is an excuse for
Not looking, not looking,
This is my world, I made it,
I am responsible for it.
My job is to change it, change it, Change it.

March 15, 2021

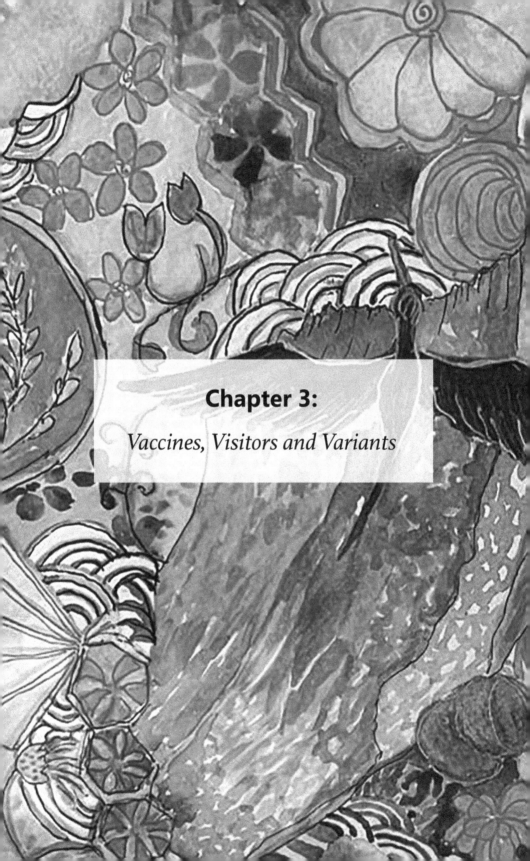

Chapter 3:

Vaccines, Visitors and Variants

All the Words are Used

All the words have been used before,
My joy has a thousand cousins and
My pain has many more.
I search for a way to say
I love you that explodes with fire
But 'love' is old and worn,
Used up before my desire.

The universe is exploding,
Stars become black holes.
Nothing lasts, and yet
That new word is waiting
In space, a supernova word
To connect old word love
With this new feeling, love.

April 1, 2021

Pandora's Box

I wonder if the ancients ever imagined
What power the stories they created
Might have on future generations.
When Pandora opened the forbidden box
Was it a warning or an invitation?

To soar high in the sky, free from earth.
Unimagined joy.
But my wings may fail and I fall
Back to my earth, "Be Careful"
The gods are warning.

There was a place of perfect harmony.
We gave it away to test our self,
To find where we belong in this wild world.
To become . . . what? Engulfed in our human
Clothes, we become part of the whole.

April 9, 2021

This is what I want to be

A refugee from the common
Neuro-pathways. Each encounter
With another will be full of possibilities,
A listening lesson in human-ness.
I will hear and see and feel,
give total attention to each offering.
Even after all this time I believe
we share more than we know,
Love still moves mountains.

April 17, 2021

Sunday Morning

Memory washes over me in waves,
Where can I hide
Who I am?

Always my Dad said
"And the hands that prepared it"
After grace. We must be grateful.

The comfortable feeling
That I created my life
Evaporates when I remember

I was surrounded by love
And faith and joy. To grow
Up and forget is the sin.

May 2, 2021

Sunday morning again

A weak sun, Grandma would say
Cold and sharp, a heavy day
My Spirit sags, my mind is slow
Yesterday is dreamlike, the glow
Of friends together, the patio
Must be imagined, warmth and joy
Seem fragile, too light to survive.

I am greedy for sunlight, and then
My spirit soars, an ancient chariot,
Pulled by a golden sun god,
Changes from gray to gold
My life. Saved again by
A river of hope, an undeserved
Gift.

May 2, 2021

So this is what they mean

Dear old body, I should have loved you more.
I took for granted the extraordinary things you did
Walking, running, driving, sleeping, working,
Days filled with purpose, thank you.

Dying is not easy, it happens inch by inch,
Suddenly the simplest is the hardest
Finger and toenails still grow, hair too
Attention must be given to the ordinary.

At the same time the morning sunshine
Breaks my heart with its beauty.
All day the red-wing blackbird's song sings,
A Mahler symphony in my mind.

There are no casual conversations.
Each encounter is a supernova of love
A chance to recognize the angel you are

May 5, 2021

Threads

I try to create a whole idea,
"Aggression is bad" seems simple
Except immediately another thought arrives.
"What about WW2? That aggression was good"
See what I mean?

Like any complex weaving, the whole cloth
Depends on each thread. I choose one thread
And start to pull it out. The cloth falls apart . . .
Or is weakened beyond repair.
Creating is hard work!

Frost spoke about the path not taken,
Each path leads to another choice
And suddenly I am standing on shaky ground.
The warp of my life controls these threads
And only I can change the weft.

May 5, 2021

Abundance

The orange in the toe of my Christmas stocking
Was the prize.
The first corn, rushed from Dad's garden to
The boiling water was summer.
So many memories are taste.
I wonder if we are constantly trying
To recreate that joy.
        Does abundance lessen pleasure?
Seasons mean nothing. The grocery has
Everything all the time. We eat the world.
Only new flavors are discussed, tried.
Heirloom, ancient, exotic, natural . . .
These describe my search.
        Too much, too much, too much
My pantry is full, cupboards packed,
Just in case. And daily the news
Tells of hunger. And I eat.
Too much, too much, too much.

May 13, 2021

God has the last laugh

Most favored nation, phrase from the past,
Describes a family free from trouble.
Aware of blessings, lavishly thrown,
Like confetti. We accepted as our due
Carefree years—health, wealth, love.

We do not need drugs, the present is good.
Benevolent to others, smug in our ignorance
Cassandra's warning—beware, beware,
That is for the less deserving, not us.
Then the meteor landed!

The underside of life, dark, slime, smells,
Pain, uncertainty, anguish—
Wait, wait.
The sun shines, birds sing,
Flowers bloom, neighbors laugh,
Now I know both worlds are the same
Have always been the same.
Waiting for me to grow up!

May 18, 2021

It is true

I did watch and knit as the wagons rolled.
Why not? She never saw my children,
Never saw the hunger,
Never saw the light leave their eyes,
Never longed for just a moment more.

I smiled as the crowns rolled,
The heads fell bloody to the floor,
Limp bodies thrown away.
Why not? They never saw my
Child's anguish nor did they care.

Vengeance is out of date.
Forgiveness is now.
Really? The old God knew some pain
Can never be forgiven, forgotten.
My child is God, ignore at your peril.

May 23, 2021

Magnets

Playing with magnets was fun
The way they flew together
On their own, seemingly magic.

The family is the same.
An illness, a crisis, feeling alone.
A chaotic, spontaneous gathering.

The words flow, love and comfort.
A hug, caress, passing pat on an arm.
"Whatever you need, I am here."

And the monster is diminished,
A way ahead seems possible.
The world is again on track.

May 29, 2021

Welcome to a Dream

At last you came, clear as a
Kodacolor print on glossy paper.
The 70-mile drive, 4 of us in the car,
Toward lights, music, people walking
Toward adventure.
Things dreamed of, real now—
Clowns and camels, glittering costumes,
Swinging high above us, dancing below—
Constantly changing as we watched in awe.
An extraordinary gift for country children.
Leaving, one last balloon begging
To go with you, the denial, and
The crashing crushing world
Returned.

June 6, 2021

Too much

It's too hot, too cold
Too wet, too dry
Too new, too old
Too low, too high
I never say
"I don't want to."
"I don't like that."
"That is boring."
Instead a lie is better.
And so I circle others,
Don't offend, seek one
Who explores the hidden
Me with curiosity and interest.

June 7, 2021

Convention

I think I look the same as always,
Wrinkled, stooped, hobbled.
I even smile, laugh, nod,
As though I am who I was.
(I am a Fury, tearing my hair and
Screaming at the Fates. How dare they?
This is MY Child, stay away. My fury will
Burn, scar, destroy every atom of you.)
Neighbors come, go, texts,
Zooms as though life goes on.
And I make believe that is possible.

June 26, 2021

Going to the movies

Saturday afternoon at the Crandon Theater
Tarzan, The Lone Ranger, an evil man with a black mustache,
Buck Rogers, bubbling lava sure to engulf our hero.
We always sat in the last four rows.
Only we could be there, as sure as catechism or school.
Our place. And the stories were pure
Black and white, no ambiguity.
I believe children deserve that time. A sane world,
Good and evil clear to see, no adults in our space.
But always waiting at home, supper ready,
Listening to the latest imaginary crisis.

July 2, 2021

Lost, really?

I was on my way to 'control' when
'Chastity belt' caught my eye,
And the race was on. I
Needed to follow this trail.
When I remembered my first
Goal, an hour had disappeared
And I had traveled through 'c.'

My Webster's, 1983 edition, is
Heavy and awkward in my hands.
A gift I had forgotten, a world
To revel in, words that say exactly what I want.

Google has an answer
for any question. The
conversation ends,
The search is over, possibilities
Float away unexplored.
A joyful discovery lost.

July 17, 2021

Hubris

The Greeks knew, a thousand years ago,
That challenging the gods is
Fraught with danger, tale after tale told
A disastrous end for the bold
Who dared.
A reminder, no matter how we start,
Our fatal flaw, our greedy heart,
Grabs more, 'deserves' our part
Of glory, fame and wealth. Too late
Our wings fall away, we fall-fail,
We're no more than human after all.

August 11, 2021

Plan ahead

I put the coroner on speed dial
Pleased to think ahead
The kids can make that call
After I am dead.

Papers are in order
Officials satisfied.
Presents for loved ones
Wrapped and tied.

Efficient rules the day,
Wasted time is now a 'sin'
Wallow in 3 days of grief
Then life again begins.

August 24, 2021

The sex talk was hard?

The sex talk loomed,
Delay,
Keep very busy, not today.
LATER!

Today the death talk with
My daughter.
STOP driving—
Hire help—
But I am very busy, not today,
LATER!

August 26, 2021

Strangers

Thanks to the driver who missed me by a mile
Thanks to the man who found my bag
Thanks to the clerk who with a smile
Found the size I missed, to the harried Mom
Who did not drag
Her child.
And
Thanks to the unseen growers, pickers, packers,
Shippers, clerks, hidden behind my meals.
Thanks to the lovers, the thinkers, the doers,
Creators of life. Thanks to the smilers, the
Compassionate ones, the healers, the
Gentle guides,
And
Thanks for astounding life with all its lessons.
I stand in awe before this gift.

September 20, 2021

If

If I am not waiting for sunrise
Will it happen?
If I am not longing for shadows
Will they appear?
If I am not sending energy to you
Will you feel the loss?
If I am not

September 27, 2021

If you had . . .

If you had a diabolical Bent
What challenge would you invent
To upend a day?
A tray
of ice cubes on a white tile floor
Bare feet add more Complexity than before.
And then to find a way
To restart your day
Is your only chore
Complaints left outside
Your door

October 7, 2021

Just suppose

Suppose this earth we hold so dear
Is only in the mind of God?
Planets, seasons, stories clearly
Are creations in a game we play.
We do not know the rules, each day
They change. Adapt we say
But long for any anchor. Maybe
This new thought might be the key
To open hope, joy, and a serene
Mind. Is this the purpose I long to
Find? The puzzle piece that holds
Us all together.

October 13, 2021

A perfect day

Remember that summer day
All the family arrived at the cottage,
Beds, bunk house packed with
Relatives, tentative, city and country,
To honor the ancient ones?

To the wild raspberry patch,
Coffee cans wired to belts, the first plink
Of the day.
Hot, bees, sweat, scratches, bears?
And back home weary but . . .
Remove the leaves, inchworms, green ones.
Grandma made cobbler, the aunts made jam,
The kids were in the water, uncles slept.

And then a storm came, black and purple,
Wild wind, slashing rain.
On the dock, I was washed clean
A real baptism, and then
Through the starry night to
Blessed sleep.

October 19, 2021

Our food

My long-awaited cranberry sauce
was bubbling on the stove,
Aroma spilled, filled
The hall and drove me
To offer berries to my friend.
"We don't eat those."

It was the 'we' that stunned me.
How comforting to have a 'we' that
Includes me. Her filter screened
Out berries—scarlet, red, blue—it
Must be true, because her
Group said so. Done.

Could the group be wrong?
Almost too strong a question
and yet, and yet
Might breaking free be
The truth I need to feel,
To become real?

November 14, 2021

Do you wonder

Do you wonder how we
Meet each day with hope,
joy in the sunrise, expecting
Wonderful surprises?
How we cope,
battered, bruised,
By news, still await dawn
Excited by another chance
For joy. This must be
The miracle we wish for,
Happening every day.

November 27, 2021

Grasshopper

In the fable, I get a bad rap.
For one thing, I always have a sappy smile.
Ant is sober, dutiful, controlled, he
Follows a map.
Life happens while he races
To meet his needs. But
My songs fill the sky,
I sing for joy, love, hope.
But then the lesson,
"Left out in the cold, alone.
Be like the ant."

That can't be right,
Beauty, love, joy, hope
We can choose, hurrah.

December 6, 2021

Morning

The room is cold, my bed is warm,
This might be the day
I quit.
Thoughtless tasks wait
Endlessly filling space, time.
I quit.
My world is/was a dream
It seems impossible to fit.
I quit.
If not for you I joyfully would
But an aura of hope still shines.
I will try.

December 16, 2021

Alone/lonely?

In Dicken's *Christmas Carol* there is a line
"When want is more keenly felt"
No better way to bring this feeling
Forward.
After a holiday filled with
action, music, newly discovered Zoom,
The quiet, like a heavy blanket, pushes
Me down into my self . . . loss, loss, loss
One after the other till there is nothing left.
Family, friends, even my books fail
To lift the weight that slows, then stops
Hope.

December 26, 2021

STOP!

Lear, you old fool,
Did your need for love
Blind you. Your only tool
Was power. You gave that away.
Now truly blind
Can you see, must it
Take a catastrophe?
Only a story
Can break open the
Hardest heart.
Ignore the mind, start
A new path. Your last chance
To be loved/to love.

January 7, 2022

Cracks in everything

Leonard Cohen is a genius
He wrote "There is a crack in everything."
We sing his song and then
Our solid ground cracks open
And we fall again into despair.
What seemed fertile ground
(Same goals, ideals, hopes)
Becomes yet another desert.
Instead of awe, we judge,
Instead of love, we sneer,
Instead of compassion, we enjoy
The other's pain.
It is hard work to grow up!

January 15, 2022

Cleanliness is . . .

We learned this with the air we breathed,
Pick up, clean up, put away, start the day
In order, the only way.
When the house is ready, the mind can
Follow.
To create whole cloth, the warp and weft
Must begin with order, then they can hold
Our dreams, more exciting than we
Knew, a lifetime of open-eyed wonder
Is here, grab it, hold on, never
Let go.

January 20, 2022

It's all about redemption

It's all about redemption, right?
Every story, every song, every poem.
I try and fail, try and fail to reach the
Heights I dream of, to be the hero
Of my life but like Icarus I forget
That pride hides flaws, I must be
Redeemed/reminded.
Old-fashioned words,
Old-fashioned idea, any truth
For this wild world?
I wonder.

January 25, 2022

Just suppose

Let's both agree to believe,
Just for this short moment, that
We have a Marley in our past, he
Hovers, achingly silent, waits to see
Us burst open, leave
Behind our ego, answer why we
Feel incomplete, unfinished, longing to be
Better.
Suppose the lesson is that we
Are where we are meant to be,
Who we are meant to be, love/live
Life in serene joy. Possible?

February 19, 2022

I found the answer!

I found the answer,
Simple really.
I have been trying to put
The puzzle together
But the picture on the box
Doesn't match the pieces I have.
"Find the edges," experts say
That means a smooth piece
Will anchor one side. Really?
What if there are more than
Four sides? No up or down, light or dark,
Right or wrong.
What if I change my mind, accept the
Abstract picture
Is my life. Or maybe fiction is the only
Possible answer.
Or maybe I ask the wrong question.

February 25, 2022

Heroes

Amazing I loved comic books,
Hid them from my Mother, made friends
Where they were allowed, looked
For heroes in vain. Billowing cape, masks,
Flying through the air to the rescue.
Brave in the face of danger.

And here they are, our neighbors,
Struggling with illness,
Bravely standing with the outcast,
Comforting those in need.
Loving the unlovable.

No other heroes are possible.

March 24, 2022

Rage

I want to have a tongue sharpened,
Swift as a rapier, searching for his
Jugular, longing to bring excruciating pain,
Unrelenting till revelation-remorse-redemption
Come crashing down.
This old man is blind, is ignorant, is fearful.
His days are numbered,
Retribution surely stands ahead.
Dickens is right, hell waits for him.
Revelation without power, hurray!
The meaning of respect and dignity
Stood there,
Never a need to act or even
Answer ignorance.

March 25, 2022

Note: Written about Supreme Court hearings on Ketanji Brown
Jackson nomination

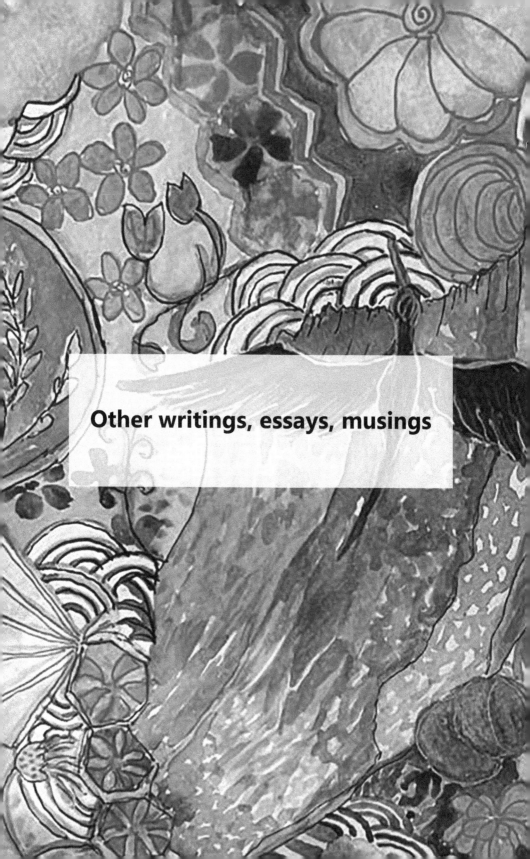

Other writings, essays, musings

My creed

I bristle at phrases like "royal family" and "First Lady." There are no royals and firsts, only people who fell into unearned and, in many cases, undeserved spots in the world, created by some unfathomable human desire to believe they may be "better." I believe America had a chance, long ago, to eliminate these beliefs, to allow a space for each person to find their own royal self. No question, it was a rocky road, lots of injustice, bad decisions, backtracking. But that little flame of an idea was there, maybe for the first and last time in history.

It is easier to give my power to someone—religious, political, mystical—than to struggle thoughtfully toward a clear understanding of who/what/where I am at this moment, knowing that understanding changes constantly. I believe the power of radicalism comes from a desire not to do the work that life offers us.

November 4, 2015

Thrashing

When I was 8-9, we would go out to the farm to help with the harvesting of hay. That was before rural electrification so . . . kerosene lamps, party telephone lines (you could listen in on your neighbor's phone calls), coal furnaces, and wood stoves in the kitchen. It was a hard workday for the grownups but an exciting playday for us. This is what I remember about those days.

Noon . . . the pump handle in the yard shrieked as the harvesters washed off the morning's dust-caked eyes and nose, face a streaked mask, hair wet and finger combed.
The young men stripped off shirts wet and salty, letting the cold water run over their heads and splashing back, chest and shoulders with the cold water, taking turns pumping for each other. A towel hung on a hook by the back door, gray and sopping wet.
Into the dining room, they spoke in monosyllables about the heat, the dust, the condition of the hay, prospects for the afternoon. Seated around the table, bare skin already sweat-shining.

As if by magic, the women appear bearing heavy platters of fried chicken and fried pork chops, bowls of mashed potatoes, brown gravy, vegetables in a rainbow of glorious color, a steady stream of food coming from the kitchen until at last a pause, everyone seems satisfied. Now dessert . . . chocolate cake with fudge frosting, lazy-daisy cake with broiled coconut & brown sugar frosting, angel food cake made with fresh egg whites and apple pie and finally more strong hot coffee poured from a blue enamel pot. The men head outside to the shade of the barn, waiting for the harvester to start again.

Now the children and women begin to eat, some at the table, some standing in the kitchen, plates in hand, planning the attack on the chaos. Children take scraps out to the chickens and pigs. Milk, butter and cream to the icehouse, the smell of wet sawdust. Dishes washed and stacked, leftovers on the table covered with white ironed napkins, floors swept, surfaces shining and clean, at last peace descends on the farmhouse, the quiet conversation that happens after hours of cooperative labor.

The sun was beginning to leave the top of the sky, shadows were lengthening, the children had carried buckets of water out to the fields and returned subdued. The noise of the harvester seemed to fade, as a cool breeze began and then the workday was over. Again the sound of the pump handle up and down, splashing water on the stone, quiet talk about the next day's farm, a drifting away of families and finally an empty kitchen. While Uncle John strolled out to survey his fields, calculating the success of the harvest, the children, worn out at last, played Monopoly on the cool parlor floor. Aunt Cloma packed leftovers to send home with her sisters, the last people to leave the kitchen. And the day was over.

October 6, 2015

In my life

Born in 1929, flapper era, stock market high, and the crash, the depression of the '30s. Living in a small town of 2000 people, no money so barter was common. Coming home to find a chicken in a gunny sack at the back door, payment for dental work. An orange in our Christmas stocking was a great treat. Canning chickens for the winter on Grandma Ison's wood stove at the farm. Luckier than city kids, everyone saw them bringing free county groceries home in their wagons. Beggars and gypsies at the back door begging for food; Mom was always afraid of them. Relatives coming back to the farm from the city, always one or two extra men sleeping in the milk house or shed. Then about '33, Germany invaded Poland and American factories started hiring workers, money started to come back in circulation, young men moved back to the cities because they could find work. By the '40s, war fever had started in earnest, December 7 and Pearl Harbor, 7 of the Crandon High School seniors enlisted, three of them were killed. Grandma Duff had a flag with 4 blue stars in her window, four sons in the service. My dad, Grandpa Ison, volunteered, was sent to Camp Chafee in Arkansas, worked on young draftees who had never been to a dentist. Sent to a hospital ship bringing wounded soldiers home from Europe and when that part was over, the ship sailed through the Panama Canal heading for the war in the Pacific. But in 1945, it was over. Dad came back home, sick with infected legs but mostly from all he had seen.

April 2, 2016

Inventions that changed the world

TV Trays

The '50s were amazing. The high school athlete I might have married was killed in a raid over Germany, in fact almost the whole high school basketball team died during the war. So along with thousands of others in their 20s, longing for a husband, children and a home, I married. But then the Korean War came along and off the men went again to war.

The GI Bill, tract housing, whole new suburbs filled former farm fields. And we were fertile, 3 or 4 babies in quick succession, jobs, wives and children, without a car, turned yards into playgrounds and kitchens into therapy offices. And then . . .

Television sets became affordable. One by one the living rooms were lit by blue light as watching became the new exercise. We bought a TV, excusing the expense because Rick had scarlet fever and needed to rest but in reality, it was a status symbol. Inviting neighbors over to watch TV became the new social event. Then TV tray tables arrived and now the invitation included a TV dinner.

Up to that time, eating supper (or dinner) at the kitchen table when Dick got home from work happened every single day, no fast food then, so preparing the meal, serving it, and cleaning up filled early evening. These hours were time to share what was happening with each of us. Rushing to the "Evening News" and then an entertainment show ended that practice.

Was our social web destroyed by television, did loss of daily family meals cause the breakdown of society, when everyone had TV their family could just stay home and watch . . . we didn't wonder about 'what if' till now, no answers.

October 25, 2019

For Katherine

Thinking about when you were born; never had there been such excitement and joy in the family. And a family reunion was planned a few months later and you were the star, of course.

Looking at one of my prized possessions, an album your Mom created for me, with pictures of all three of you dear ones reminds me that you are now a young adult with a life I can barely imagine. Your world is changing almost as much as you are, exciting and scary at the same time.

Trying to remember a song I heard, something about 'you have a friend in me' and I hope you know that is and will always be true, if you ever need/want anything I will be there for you.

Happy Birthday.
Love,
Nana

November 14, 2019

Noreen Rae Cook

In a small Northern Wisconsin town,
    Surrounded by lumber and farms,
        amid self-sufficient families,
        a newly graduated dentist and his wife have their first child . . .
And the stock market crashes, the Great Depression arrives,
    then just when things start to look hopeful—
    WWII tears the town's families apart,
        scattering the future all over the world.

The child is me—Noreen Rae Ison
    I might have had a predicted life but once the box is open,
        change happens.
Surrounded by love and also high expectations,
    I went to UW-Madison, and married,
    Then, after my husband returned from service in the Philippines,
    back to Madison with two children, on husband's GI Bill,
    and then the 1960s, with one more child,
    I felt buried in suburbia.

Inevitably life changed, divorce and belated career, retirement, travel
    all interspersed with marriages, births, deaths.
Now I am 92. Still can't believe it, but every morning I wake
    filled with inexpressible joy and gratitude.

CPSIA information can be obtained
at www.ICGtesting.com
Printed in the USA
BVHW062234250522
637684BV00004B/16

9 781645 383536